HOW A KID WITH $0 CREATED NIKE

Mitchell Hazlewood
Eric Smith

1 Down Publication

1 Down
PUBLICATION

INTRODUCTION

The story of Nike - this Nike documentary tells the history of Nike, starting with Nike founder Phil Knight first imagining the idea of importing Japanese running shoes. We'll look at the struggles Phil had building his company, dealing with suppliers, and handing controversies Nike was involved in. We'll also look at how Nike started out as Blue Ribbon Sports, but why they changed their name and brand to Nike. We'll even cover Nike's IPO and selling their shares on the stock market. There's plenty of entrepreneurial lessons and marketing strategies in this inspiring business success story - but as with any big company, there's also a darker side. This book aims to cover the full story of Nike, the rise of Phil Knight's business empire.

It all began while working on an assignment to invent a new business. On a piece of paper Phil Knight wrote: "Can Japanese Sports Shoes Do to German Sports Shoes What Japanese Cameras Did to German Cameras?" You see, Phil had noticed how two Japanese camera companies, Nikon and Canon, had replaced German cameras in the market which used to be more dominant, and he wondered if the same thing could happen with running shoes. Now at the time, two German companies, Adidas and Puma were the leading running shoe brands in America, and they had a very strong hold of the market. But Phil Knight had heard the Japanese were experimenting with some new shoe designs, and he also knew that it would be cheaper to produce shoes in Japan as well.

So Phil got extremely invested in this assignment for his business class, and genuinely started to believe there was a great business opportunity here to import Japanese shoes into the American market. But when Phil presented this to the class, nobody else seemed to see it that way. He even told some of his friends about the idea, but none of them seemed to pay much attention either. Of course, if Phil did want to actually pursue this idea himself, he knew how difficult it would be. He didn't know anyone in Japan to reach out to, and he knew absolutely nothing about importing Japanese shoes, or even how to sell them in America for that matter. So, could he really just do it?

CHAPTER 1: FINDING PURPOSE

"First year of sales for 1964 we sold $8000 - we made a $240 profit."

*Today his company Nike have grown in 30
billion dollars in sales last year"*

"Michael Jordan in the NBA"

Phil Knight suddenly woke up. He'd just been having a nightmare where his life had no purpose. Except, it wasn't just a dream. This was his reality. Unsure what to do with his life, Phil went to the University of Oregon where he studied Journalism and developed his interest in running. It was here that he met with the track coach Bill Bowerman, a famous coach in America who'd trained olympic athletes. Phil trained under Bowerman as a middle-distance runner, and the two men struck up a great friendship. They didn't know it at the time, but that friendship would later become the foundation of the biggest sports company in the world. But, we'll get to that.

After graduating with a journalism degree in 1959, Phil was still very confused about what to do with his life.Deep down, he'd wanted to become an athlete, but at 24 years old he had to admit it: the dream was dead. Despite all his lessons and training at college, he just hadn't got to the level needed. And now, he felt lost. Phil even enlisted in the army and completed a year of service thinking that might give him a sense of direction. It didn't. He was left frustrated and angry. So, after the army, Phil enrolled in the Graduate School of Business at Stanford University. And it was here at Stanford that he finally found his calling. While working on an assignment to invent a new business, Phil had an idea that would change his life forever. On a piece of paper he wrote:

"Can Japanese Sports Shoes Do to German Sports Shoes What Japanese Cameras Did to German Cameras?"

You see, Phil had noticed how two Japanese camera companies, Nikon and Canon, had replaced German cameras in the market which used to be more dominant, and he wondered if the same thing could happen with running shoes. Now at the time, two german companies, Adidas and Puma were the leading running shoe brands in America, and they had a very strong hold of the market.   But Phil had heard the Japanese were experimenting with some new shoe designs, and he also knew that it would be cheaper to produce shoes in Japan as well. So Phil got extremely invested in this assignment for his business class, and genuinely started to believe there was a great business opportunity here to import Japanese shoes into the American market.

But when Phil presented this to the class, nobody else seemed to see it that way. He even told some of his friends about the idea, but none of them seemed to pay much attention either. Of course, if Phil did want to actually pursue this idea himself, he knew how difficult it   would be. He didn't know anyone in Japan to reach out to, and he knew absolutely nothing about importing Japanese shoes, or even how to sell them in America for that matter. So, could he really just do it?

CHAPTER 2: A TRIP TO THE FUTURE

After graduating from business school in 1962, Phil found himself back at home living with his parents. That familiar feeling was back that his life was just passing him by, and he needed to do something meaningful. One day, Phil finally decided he couldn't just keep waiting for some magic opportunity, and he had to go and create an opportunity for himself. So, Phil and one of his friends decided to take a long trip to go travelling round the world. Phil had stayed obsessed with his idea of bringing Japanese shoes to the American market, and so he figured as part of the trip he would visit Japan to see if he could make his crazy idea into a reality. But first, they visited classic European cities, backpacked through Asia, and even stopped in Greece, where Phil saw the Temple of Athena Nike, dedicated to the goddess of Victory.

Phil and his friend then went to Hawaii, and that's where things changed. Phil and his friend surfed, relaxed on the beach, and loved the whole place so much they ended up getting jobs in Honolulu selling encyclopaedias door to door, simply so they could afford to stay in this Hawaiian paradise a little longer. However Phil was pretty shy and didn't do well at the sales job at all, and eventually he decided he'd done enough relaxing and it was time to leave. His friend had met a girl and stayed behind though, so Phil said goodbye, and continued his trip alone. And Phil already knew exactly where he wanted to go next. It was time to get serious about his dream. It was time to go to Japan.

In 1962, in the City of Kobe, Phil came across one particular running shoe that caught his eye. The brand was called Tiger, and the shoes were manufactured by a company known as Onitsuka. Not only did he like the design, the shoes ticked the two main criteria Phil needed: they were clearly high quality shoes, and yet they were relatively cheap. Phil liked the shoe so much that he cold called the owners of the shoe brand, and managed to arrange a meeting. Feeling both nervous and excited, Phil put on a suit, and went to meet the manufacturers of the Japanese shoe he liked so much.

Before going he bought a copy of 'How to Do Business with the Japanese' and memorised as much information as he could. Despite Phil having zero expertise in the business, he introduced himself at the meeting as an American shoe distributor who was going to help market their shoes in America. It turns out that Onitsuka had been looking for a way to sell its shoes in America already. So they were actually very excited when Phil came to them with the same idea.

5

Perhaps that's why they were willing to overlook the fact that Phil looked like he was fresh out of university - which he quite literally was. But despite being a recent graduate in his 20s with no actual experience of running a business, Phil had memorised lots of facts and statistics about the American shoe market from his assignment at university, and so he was basically able to recite parts of his presentation during the meeting, and so it looked like he completely knew what he was talking about. The Japanese managers were impressed. However, one of them asked Phil a very simple question: *'what's the name of the company you're from?'* Phil suddenly felt his heart beating faster.

Of course the truth was, Phil didn't have a company name because he didn't actually have a company yet. He just had this crazy idea to import Japanese shoes to America. Phil's mind started racing - for a split second he felt completely out of his depth and just wanted to be back at home with his parents - and that's when his mind suddenly flashed to the blue ribbons from his childhood that he used to have hung up on his wall. After a second pause, Phil replied: *"Gentlemen, I represent Blue Ribbon Sports of Portland, Oregon."* He just kind of blurted the name out of nowhere, since in truth he'd never expected to get this far.

But after inventing a company name on the spot, Phil could feel his confidence increasing. He went onto explain the size of the American market and how Onitsuka's Tiger shoes were different to what they had in America, meaning there was a huge opportunity if Onitsuka and him teamed up. The Japanese company were so keen, they basically began pitching Phil, and asked him if he would be their distribution partner in the US - to which Phil obviously agreed. And then he asked them to ship over some samples to his address in America. It seemed like Phil's crazy idea was about to become a reality.

CHAPTER 3: ONE BECOMES TWO

One month. Two months. Three months. Four months. The time kept passing, and no shoe samples arrived. Phil couldn't understand it; he'd returned to America so excited and optimistic, because it seemed like his meeting with the Japanese shoe manufacturer had gone so well. So, he wrote to them to find out what was going on with the samples he'd been promised, which he'd paid $50 for. He got a letter back saying: *"Shoes coming, In just a little more days."*

Phil was back at his parents house, and so he showed the letter to his dad who just chuckled, and said *'Son, that fifty bucks is long gone.'* Had Phil really been scammed? Depressed, Phil went and got a job to try and make some money - he ended up working as an accountant, but he didn't really like it. And then suddenly one morning, twelve sample pairs of shoes from Japan arrived at his doorstep! They were finally here, and it was worth the wait - they were just like he'd hoped. Phil was so excited that he went to see his old running coach Bill Bowerman to show him the new shoes and see what he thought.

Bowerman was highly respected in the world of running and he'd always been obsessed with improving athlete's shoes. In fact, back when Phil was at university with him, he'd notice Bowerman take student's shoes and cut them open and make adjustments - for example adding more cushion or using more lightweight materials - and then stitching them back together. Sometimes his experiments just made their feet painful, but quite often Bowerman improved the shoes and made them better or more comfortable for running.

One thing was for sure: Bowerman really knew his stuff when it came to running shoes, and that's why Phil was so keen to hear his opinion on his new Japanese running shoes. Surprisingly, Bowerman liked the sample shoes so much that he offered to be Phil's business partner! And Bowerman was basically the perfect partner to have - he'd spent his life on the track training athletes, was one of the most experienced track coaches with countless records, and he was obsessed with the construction of track shoes.

BLUE RIBBON SPORTS

So, Phil and Bowerman agreed to be co-founders of the new company Blue Ribbon Sports, with both of them investing $500 each into their new company. And all that money was used to order 300 pairs of shoes from Japan, at a price of roughly $3.33 a pair. Phil also wrote a letter to Onitsuka asking if Blue Ribbon Sports could be the exclusive distributor of these Tiger shoes in the western United States. They agreed, and shortly after, in April 1964, a shipment of 300 Tiger shoes arrived from Japan.

Phil now had a shoe supplier, a business partner, and hundreds of shoes to sell. There was just one problem.What Phil didn't have was anywhere to sell the shoes. You see when Phil went to all of the local sporting goods stores to see if they'd stock the shoe, they didn't take Phil seriously - and said they had no need for another track shoe. So, Phil realised he was going to have to sell these shoes himself...

CHAPTER 4: BLUE RIBBON

Phil had 300 pairs of shoes to sell, so he began going to track meets and running clubs, and started selling the shoes from the trunk of his car. He would enthusiastically show the shoes to runners, coaches and fans at the running track. His commitment and drive, together with Bowerman's connections, saw them sell out all 300 pairs within just 3 months.

It was interesting because in the past when Phil had tried sales he'd failed horribly - but that was when he was selling encyclopaedias door to door. When it came to these running shoes, selling them seemed strangely easy - and Phil felt that was because customers could sense his personal belief in the product - his conviction that these shoes genuinely were better than the alternatives made people want to buy them. Plus, clearly there was demand for these high quality shoes at an affordable price, as by the end of their first year, Blue Ribbon Sports had sold $8000 worth of shoes. And so Phil used the money he'd made to order 900 more pairs from Japan. Shortly after this they recruited some sales reps, mostly ex-runners who shared the vision of what the company was trying to do, and who worked solely on commission - they'd get $2 for every pair of shoes they sold, and so they drove all over America to every high school and college track meet that they could.

Courtesy of Nike

This success allowed Phil to get a business loan from the bank, so they could move Blue Ribbon Sports out of Phil's parent's basement, and into its first real office. However since Bowerman still had a full-time job, Phil decided to hire the company's first full-time employee, Jeff Johnson, the man who would later go on to come up with the company's iconic name, Nike. But for now, they were still called Blue Ribbon Sports.

And with sales rising rapidly, in 1966 they were able to open their own retail store to sell their shoes. A clever move they made was they designed the store to be a sanctuary for runners - a place that they could hang out and talk, and browse shelves full of books related to running, which helped them attract a lot of attention. And whilst Phil and the new employee Johnson worked on the Business side of the operations, Bowerman was handling the creative side of things. For example, Bowerman began to tinker with the shoe designs. Once a shipment arrived from Japan, he would take a few shoes and rip them apart to see how they were designed. Once he'd studied the shoe, he would make notes on how to improve them. These notes were then sent to the manufacturer in Japan asking for changes to be made before the next shipment. You could say that Bowerman was basically now designing Onitsuka's shoes for them. Around this time, Bowerman also started coaching popular runners and future Olympians, helping to build their brand further and sell even more shoes. And not just that, but Bowerman almost single-handedly made jogging popular.

You see, back in the 60's jogging was not a mainstream exercise at all, but Bowerman wrote a book about it that surprisingly sold over a million copies and helped kickstart the popularity of jogging. Which of course, meant more people were in need of jogging shoes, and what better place to buy them than the company of the man who'd popularised jogging in the first place?

In fact, one of Bill's shoe designs, called The Cortez, became the highest selling shoe in 1969, with Blue Ribbon making a total revenue of around $300,000. So, business was booming, and everything seemed to be going great between Phil's company Blue Ribbon Sports and Onitsuka in Japan. Together, they had created a partnership that brought success to both parties. But what Phil didn't know was that Onitsuka was planning to stab them in the back.

CHAPTER 5: BETRAYAL

Phil asked Onitsuka if Blue Ribbon Sports could be the exclusive distributor for Tiger shoes across all of America, not just the west like previously agreed. But they initially said no, because they didn't think Phil's company was big or established enough to handle that, and they wanted someone with offices on the East coast. On the spot, Phil immediately said: *'but we do have offices on the east coast'*. In reality, they didn't, but Onitsuka believed Phil, and was impressed that Blue Ribbon seemed like a much bigger company than they'd realised. So they struck a deal for Blue Ribbon to be the exclusive US partner for the Tiger brand shoes, and Phil ordered 20,000 more pairs.

The executive from Onitsuka told him he'd ship them to Blue Ribbon's East Coast office. Which of course, they didn't really have. So after the meeting, to try and raise money for these new offices, Phil sent out fliers advertising the chance for people to invest in Blue Ribbon Sports. They said it was a fast growing shoe company looking to expand, and people could buy shares. Then they sat back and waited for people to invest. But, nobody at all responded. It was humiliating, and also extremely worrying that nobody seemed to believe in the potential of their business, as nobody at all wanted to invest theirmoney.

The only money they did get was from the parents of one of Blue Ribbon's early employees, Bob Woodell. His parents knew the company desperately needed money, and offered to put in $8000, which was literally their entire life savings. It drained their balance to almost zero, and put them in a very difficult financial situation, but they wanted to do what they could to give the company the best chance of survival. Phil didn't want to take their money, but the banks were refusing to loan him any more, and so he had no other real choice.

On the plus side, Phil and Bowerman both loved the shoes created by Onitsuka. They respected the quality of the Japanese brand, and of course it seemed win-win for both sides, because thanks to their company Blue Ribbon Sports, Onitsuka had now become a formidable brand in the United States. So, Phil understandably thought that the future of his company was with Onitsuka. But the truth is, they had some problems, and they were about to get even bigger. You see, the initial success of Blue Ribbon Sports had led to the rapid opening of new stores, which often left Phil in a risky situation where he constantly had to worry about cash flow to support the increase in stores and employees. Phill had to get more facilities, hire more staff and order more shoes. The Cortez for example had quickly become the most popular shoes in America and they were selling out faster than they could keep up with. So Phil repeatedly tried to have Onitsuka send the shoes faster to meet the demand, but the Japanese brand continued to send them at the same pace.

It was only later that Phil found out that Onitsuka had been selling to their Japanese customers first as the priority, and simply importing whatever was left over to the US. It was unfair, but there wasn't really much Phil could do. To compound the situation, Onitsuka was slow to produce the suggestions and innovations that Phil and Bowerman shared with them, and sometimes, they completely ignored their suggestions - which infuriated Bowerman who'd been working hard on new designs and improvements. So, hoping to improve the situation with their supplier, and discuss renewing their contract, Phil arranged another in-person meeting with a representative from Onitsuka, a man Kitami. But the meeting was strange - Kitami said blue ribbon sales were disappointing, and didn't seem that interested in renewing a long-term deal with Blue Ribbon.

Phil couldn't understand it; he felt his company had definitely earnt the contract extension. After all, Onitsuka's success in the United States was down to Blue Ribbon Sports. They'd introduced the Tiger brand in America, and sales were growing every year. Phil even showed them a survey that revealed that 70 percent of American runners wore or owned one of their shoes. Not to mention that Bowerman had helped improve their shoe designs.

Phil had already been a little suspicious that Onitsuka were planning to make partnerships with other distributors, and it was becoming increasingly clear that something wasn't right. So, when Kitami left the room, Phil took a folder out of his briefcase. It contained a list of 18 athletic shoe distributors across the US, and a schedule of appointments to meet them. It was now clear that Onitsuka was secretly plotting to replace Blue Ribbon and find a new distributor.

From their perspective, now that they'd gained a significant foothold in the United States thanks to Blue Ribbon's efforts, the Onitsuka executives decided that they needed to move on to more experienced distributors to expand and increase their revenue. Phil was outraged, but most of all he was hurt. He confronted them about this, and pointed out they still had a contract in place for at least another year. However the Japanese brand then gave Phil an ultimatum. Either we buy 51% of Blue Ribbon Sports, or otherwise we make deals with other distribution partners.

Phil Knight immediately rejected their offer to buy his company - he didn't want to sell, and he couldn't believe this was happening.But, Phil knew there was really only one way forward now. If Onitsuka were going to start partnering with other American distributors, then it was time for war.

CHAPTER 6: DON'T GET ANGRY, GET EVEN

It took a little while for Phil to get over the shock of everything that had gone down in the meeting, but when he did, he decided to strike back. Phil and Bowerman realised that losing the Onitsuka Tiger brand wasn't necessarily the end of the world - in fact, maybe this was an opportunity. They could be so much more than just a distributor. After all, the Cortez, Onitsuka's best selling shoe, was Bowerman's design. So, why couldn't Blue Ribbon just make their own shoes and sell them? Plus that way, they wouldn't have to keep waiting for shipments to arrive, and they could make as many shoes as they wanted. So, the two co-founders gathered the whole team together and began working on creating their own original shoes, instead of selling Onitsuka's Tiger shoes.

But first, they needed a new name. Phil initially wanted to call their new brand Dimension Six, but pretty much nobody else liked that name. And then Jeff Johnson, their first employee, said an idea had suddenly come to him in a dream the previous night: let's call it Nike. Phil just looked at him blankly, and said *'what?'* *"'It's the Greek winged goddess of victory,'* Johnson explained. Phil thought back to the temple he'd visited whilst travelling. He had to admit, the connection to victory certainly made a lot of sense for a sports brand, but the truth was that Phil himself actually wasn't that keen on the name Nike at first. But the problem was, they were running out of time and had to decide on a name right now, because they needed to start making plans for their new shoe brand as soon as possible. So, left with few other options, Phil agreed to go with the name Nike.

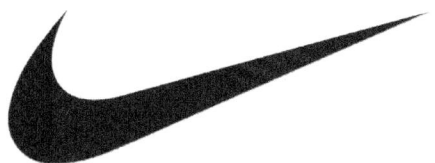

Next up, they needed a logo. So they recruited a graphic design student from a nearby university to create it, and she came up with the now-iconic swoosh. She got paid just $35 for it. But now that the name and logo were sorted out, there was one more crucial thing they needed to do to really take the fight to Onitsuka. Phil needed a shoe manufacturer who could produce their new high quality shoes at an affordable price.

They already had the design they wanted to use for their first shoe with the Nike logo, which was basically a new version of the popular Cortez. But they had to find the right manufacturer to make it. And all the initial manufacturers they tested seemed to have quality control issues.

At a company meeting, Phil told his employees: *"Our partnership with Onitsuka is over, and we're completely on our own now. We have this new line we're working on which we're calling Nike, but there are big problems with the quality. We're trying to get it fixed, but we don't have much time so there's no margin for error."* Phil looked down the table at the employees in the meeting and realised everyone was slumped in their seats, looking defeated, as if losing their deal with Onitsuka meant the end of Blue Ribbon Sports. Phil realised he needed to inspire his team, and so he pivoted his speech, and said: *"So . . . in other words, "This is the moment we've been waiting for."* Everyone around the table looked up, and Phil continued: *"No more selling someone else's brand. Onitsuka has been holding us down for years. Their late deliveries, their mixed-up orders, their refusal to hear and implement our design ideas — Let's not look at this as a crisis.*

Let's look at this as our liberation."

As Phil stopped speaking he could sense a wave of relief around the table. The mood had changed after Phil's speech, and the employees felt that maybe, just maybe, this wasn't the end of the company at all. They got to work on how they could make this new Nike brand successful, and how they could partner with the right manufacturers. Although Phil made sure he didn't make the same mistake he'd made with Onitsuka. So, rather than committing to just one manufacturer, he established a network of manufacturers, which gave him full control over production. That wasn't quite the end of their dealings with Onitsuka though, as they actually sued Blue Ribbon Sports, claiming that starting this new Nike brand breached their contract which stated Blue Ribbon would only sell Tiger shoes. Phil then counter-sued that Onitsuka had actively been trying to break its exclusivity deal with Blue RIbbon Sports. In the end, both parties eventually settled and went their separate ways.

In 1971, the company Blue Ribbon Sports officially became Nike, and by this point, the company had crossed a million dollars in sales per year - and from then onwards, Nike's expansion skyrocketed as they began to grow into the most famous sports brand we know and recognise today. At the 1972 Olympics Nike featured heavily, giving them a lot of exposure on a global stage. Revenue rose rapidly to $14 million in 1976, and then doubled in just one year to $28 million in 1977. Around that time, Phil opened new factories around the world, and continued to reinvest everything in more growth. And it was working. Nike was on a huge upswing. They weren't only gaining market share, but they were also fast becoming a fashion statement. However, their success was being envied by a lot of American brands who were watching very closely, waiting for their moment to strike the company down.

CHAPTER 7: NIKE VS THE GOVERNMENT

Things seemed to be going great for Nike - sales were amazing, word of mouth was positive and their legal disputes were behind them. The only slight problem was they were actually still quite cash poor. Phil was reinvesting every penny he could back into more growth, and even borrowing money to help ramp up expansion faster. To him, it was grow or die. So he kept ordering more and more shoes, opening more stores, and hiring more employees. To help fund this expansion, Phil was thinking about taking the company public. But then one morning he got a letter that changed everything.

It was a bill from the US customs service, saying Nike owed them $25 million dollars. At first Phil thought it must be a joke or some strange mistake. If they actually did owe $25 million to the government, they'd be out of business. It would be all over just like that - everything they'd worked for. After a few phone calls, it soon became clear that the bill was completely real. And the actual reason behind it was something surprisingly sinister.

What had happened was that Nike's American competitors, Keds,

Converse and a few small factories - were getting scared of Nike's popularity and growth. They saw Nike as a threat that could potentially shut them out of the market. So, they sent representatives to Washington and lobbied the customs office to effectively put a stop to Nike's growth by enforcing something called 'American Selling Price'. ASP was an archaic rule from before The Great Depression, that said that if there is a shoe manufactured by a company in the US, then anyone importing a similar shoe from abroad must pay an import duty of 20% of the competitors selling price.

The whole idea behind this law was to promote nationalism, and essentially prevent companies from importing products that could be made in America. And Nike's competitors had lobbied the federal government to enforce this old rule. You see, because Nike wasn't manufacturing its shoes in America but in Japan, their competitors realised all they needed to do was make a copy of Nike's shoes and make them extremely expensive. By doing that, they had successfully created an American alternative, and even though Nike's shoes were the original thing, because Nike's products were being imported from another country, they got hit with ridiculously high import fees because of this American Selling Price rule. This basically meant Phil would have to pay an additional $6 on every pair they imported.

To make matters much worse, the import duties were backdated three years on every pair of shoes Nike had imported - which ultimately had led to the $25 million bill they received. Phil knew there was no way Nike could pay that much money - it would bankrupt them. There was only one option and that was to fight. Phil hired one of the best lawyers he could find, and for three brutal years, Phi went neck-and-neck with the Customs office and the likes of Converse and Keds in court. Nike also produced a TV commercial telling their story, and explaining what was happening to them, to try and get customers fired up and on their side. And, it worked.

Nike's competitors and their accomplices in the government realised Nike were going to fight this with everything they had, and in the end they reached a settlement of $9 million dollars instead of $25 million. Phil still thought it was outrageous, but in those 3 years the legal battle had been going on, Nike had grown tremendously, and their sales had reached a whopping $440 million. So they could now afford to settle and put the whole thing behind them. It had been another close scare, but the company had made it through stronger than ever, and now, it was time for some very good news.

CHAPTER 8: GOING PUBLIC

In 1980, Nike became a public company which effectively killed its cash flow problems completely, and allowed them to ramp up their growth even more. And since Phil alone owned a 46 percent share of the company, he became a very wealthy man. But also, remember earlier on the parents of one of Nike's early employees invested their life savings into helping the company survive when they were low on cash? Well, they hadn't done that as an investment to make money at all, they'd done it to simply try and keep the company alive. But they'd been given shares in return. And so after Nike went public, Phil had one of his happiest moments of his career, when he got to tell them that their initial $8000 investment was now worth $1.6 million dollars. That money was obviously completely life changing for them, and they couldn't believe it.

From there on, Nike became bigger and bigger. Phil signed deals with two Chinese factories which made Nike the first American shoemaker to be allowed to do business in China. They also branched out into selling clothes, and this not only helped them make more money, and attract more investors, but it also gave them an advantage when negotiating endorsement deals with athletes, as they could now offer them more than just shoes. And celebrity endorsements were actually one of Nike's biggest keys to success.

 **Tiger Woods**

 **Lebron James**

They agreed deals with rookie athletes like Tiger Woods and Lebron James in the very early stages of their career, and of course when they went onto become massive stars, it massively boosted Nike's popularity.

 **Michael Jordan**

Although their most lucrative endorsement of all was with Michael Jordan - they spotted his potential early on and signed him for a sponsorship deal back in the beginning of his career. And as Jordan rose to stardom, his shoe line, Air Jordans, went on to make hundreds of millions of dollars.

By 1986, Nike had overtaken Converse to become the biggest sports brand in America. And at this point you might be thinking that Nike is simply an incredible business success story. But here's the thing: behind all that success was a very dark secret. A secret that involved violent intimidation, slavery, harassment, and child labour. And that secret was about to be exposed.

◆ ◆ ◆

CHAPTER 9: THE DARK TRUTH

 **Jeffrey Ballinger**

It was 1991, and everyone working at Nike was having a normal day, when American labour activist Jeffery Ballinger published a report that nearly destroyed Nike's entire reputation. In his film, 'behind the swoosh', he claimed that Nike secretly used child labour and that the company exploited people living in underdeveloped countries. The video claimed that workers in these countries were forced to live in slums or near open sewers where they shared toilets and bathwater with over 100 different families. These workers were then cramped in factories which were often housed in damaged buildings that posed fire risks.

During their work hours, they were denied access to drinking water or toilets. At the end of the day, after which they had gone through all this inhumane treatment, they were paid a meagre sum of $1.25.

Then In 2001, a BBC documentary uncovered use of child labor and poor working conditions in a Cambodian factory used by Nike. The documentary focused on six girls, who all worked seven days a week, often 16 hours a day. All of these claims led to a lot of backlash, with many students and activists around the world participating in protests against Nike. Some people called for a boycott of all their products, and several universities cut ties with the shoe brand completely.

Sales dropped and Nike's stock fell by 15%, with the company being portrayed in the media as a company willing to exploit workers and deprive them of their basic wages needed to sustain themselves. Phil Knight had always been in a position where he and his company were the good guys, but this time, he was the bad guy. It was a different challenge, and he responded by promising that he would personally ensure conditions at Nike factories around the world improved. After that, Nike spent the next decade trying to fix its reputation.

Of course the truth is, the company was basically founded on the principle of finding cheaper labour abroad in order to be able to make good quality shoes that were cheaper than competitors. But to be fair, Nike definitely did make changes to significantly improve conditions for overseas workers. And many human rights activists have acknowledged their efforts to minimise these problems. But allegations never fully stopped.

A 2005 report by the company found that workers in up to half of its factories were still forced to work sixty-hour weeks, made less than minimum wage, or were denied use of bathrooms and drinking water. And even more recently in December 2021, the European Center for Constitutional and Human Rights filed a criminal complaint against Nike and other brands, alleging that they benefited from the use of forced labor in China.

Now to be fair and give the other side to this, Phil would argue that those factories involved in these scandals weren't actually Nike's, they just rented them along with other tenants - so Nike wasn't directly controlling these factories, they just made deals with them. And whilst that's not an excuse, Phil is right that singling out Nike for using sweatshops misses the bigger picture: which is that countless multinational companies use overseas labour with very questionable conditions in parts of their supply chains. Many of the items we all use every day were quite possibly produced with cheap labour in terrible working conditions. It's that if you look into almost any business deep enough, you're gonna find a darker side. But what's particularly interesting about Nike, is how they've managed to turn controversy into profit.

CHAPTER 10: TURNING CONTROVERSY INTO MILLIONS

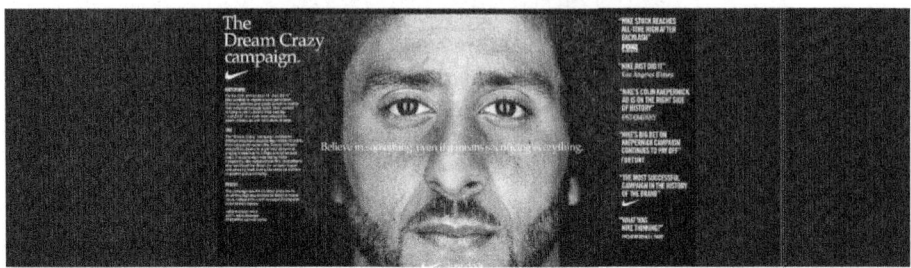

In 2018 Nike launched a new ad, titled Dream crazy, with former NFL player Colin Kaepernick as the voice and face of its new just do it campaign. Kaepernick himself posted a black and white close-up picture of his face with the words: *"Believe in something. Even if it means sacrificing everything."* That statement was in reference to a controversy that began back in 2016 when Kaepernick himself triggered a political scandal by kneeling during the US national anthem to protest against racial injustice and police brutality in America. Many people, including then President Donald Trump, claimed that Kaepernick was disrespecting the flag and the country.

So Nike's partnership with Colin was controversial to say the least - their stock price immediately fell 2.5%, and many people across the United States destroyed their Nike shoes and declared a boycott of the company. But then, something interesting happened. A lot of people who shared the same sentiment behind the theme of Nike's ad, came on their side- and many people started buying and wearing Nike's products as a show of support. Thanks to the controversial and bold marketing move, Nike got more attention than ever, and broke many records, gaining $6 billion in brand value, $163 million in media, and an additional 31% bump in sales. The campaign also earned Nike its first Emmy award since 2002 for the most outstanding commercial of 2019. In the end, all the shouts for the boycott of Nike products had little significance or any major impact on its sales. And this wasn't the first time that Nike had leaned into controversies to make more money.

In 1988, Nike released its first Just do it campaign. The campaign touched on the subject of ageism, featuring an 80-year-old marathon runner who ran 17 miles every morning. Then in February 1995, Nike released a Just do it campaign which featured a HIV-positive runner. So, why does Nike take risks in their ads that they know will create some controversy? Well the reality is Nike have an experienced marketing team that assesses the risk versus reward, and makes a calculated decision. In the case of ads like these, they weighed up the costs and believed that the benefits were worth it. And whilst many other factors obviously affect sales, it's clear that their ad campaigns have played a huge role in the company's success.

Between when the first just do it campaign launched in 1988 to 1998, Nike increased sales from 800 million dollars to 9.2 billion. However, after 40 years, Phil stepped down as CEO. His story is pretty remarkable - starting out as a kid with no experience, heading to Japan to try and make his crazy idea a reality, and ultimately building the biggest sports brand in the entire world. But, what about you? What's your crazy idea? Because if one thing is clear from Phil's story it's that the timing is never perfect, sometimes you've gotta just take a leap of faith. Or in the words of Nike, just do it.

And if you want some more business stories and lessons to inspire you, check out our other books in this Luxury Brands series, that I think you're really gonna like. I'll hopefully see you there. Thank you for reading. Cheers.

Printed in Great Britain
by Amazon

20669145R10031